BIRHTDAY ODYSSEY

By

Francis K. Offin

Where it all began

The duel of choices

The genuine surprise

Precious Memories

The preparation

I am glad you came

Dad's joy

The moment of laughter

Lyren is in charge

Mom wondered

Noble's observation

De ja vu

The climax

ACKNOWLEDGEMENT

I deeply appreciate all the people who have in diverse ways shaped my life with their exemplary life of excellence, sacrifice, love and encouragement. They are the ones who helped me see greatness in me. Foremost is the Holy Spirit of God Who has always remained my true encouragement and inspiration in life. Thank you all for your unique reinforcements and friendships.

DEDICATION

This book is primarily dedicated to Mrs. Alice Oduro, Former Headmistress of Obuasi Methodist Basic School (my alma mater), for her invaluable, multitudinous and incalculable reassurances in my education, and further dedicated to students of Adisadel College (my alma mater), and to the youth in Ghana and beyond.

PREFACE

The title of this book, 'Birthday Odyssey', came as a result of me falling in love with the word "Odyssey". It conveys a unique meaning for life. Life is a series of long adventurism, priorities and each stage must be enjoyed uniquely, and fully. The most fitting gift I thought of giving to Evelyn Asare, my cousin, one of her birthdays was a poem that suited her age and day. I thought of birthdays as an odyssey and wrote a poem covering two pages of a sheet of paper to express that idea. Unfortunately, I never had the

opportunity to present this customized gift to   her.
Eight years later, the urge came for me to rehash the poem to suit an ongoing British Broadcasting   Corporation   (BBC) competition. I spent five days on the work to meet the deadline. I did so under a lot of pressure because I was writing exams at the same time. Even though my script was not selected, all who had the opportunity to read it afterwards found it inspiring. Yielding to a persistent prompting within me, I have done my best to ready the material   for   publication.

"Friendship is a choice of decision." – The Bold.
It was lunch time at Thess-Han College of

Arts in Obuasi, in the beautiful country of Ghana, and Quamey, the closest friend of Lyren, recited a birthday poem to her at the colorfully flowery river bank of their college. They loved to be together at the river bank as this brought precious historical memories to almost every Ghanaian who happened to sit there. Ghana, according to history, was formally Gold Coast and Obuasi was factually known to be a city of gold. Obuasi is still, today, the heart of gold mining activities. How romantic the aura was! Their break time was the first four hours posterior commencement of the morning English class which started at eight. Previously, Lyren had always been bothered about the origin of birthday celebrations and the need for them. Questions flooded her curiously-philosophical mind, and she always wondered, 'is a birthday celebration a natural occurrence? Is it a deliberate creation of man? Is it for the fun of it or God ordained it? Has it any link at all to the meaning of life? Is a birthday the birth of a person's destiny?'.These were only a few questions that were thrown at him by her after reciting to Lyren his poem entitled, 'BLISS OF BIRTHDAY'. Quamey with a look of perplexity in his eyes was still thinking about the chronology of how he would answer her, and wasn't sure whether to optimize his wits and intelligence in order to do that. Meanwhile Lyren, at the same time, also tried to weigh her questions against the poem that had just been read to her. Upon consideration of her thoughts, Lyren quickly implored Quamey to read the poem again. He gladly cleared his throat to do it the second time. This time with a greater emphasis on the words and with a touching enthusiasm he read:

'You have heard it being said, that be happy
You have heard it being said, that money makes you happy
You have heard it being said, that there are lucky days for everyone
You have probably believed that happiness was not always assured
You have heard it being said, that happiness is an individual quest
Yet what could make almost everybody, to be happy with birthdays?
What could make a mother rejoice at the birth of a child?
What could make society applaud the birth of a child?
Birth must be a victory to celebrate I think, and believe
Birth must be a wonder to all people I think, and believe
Birth must be a satisfaction to the parents I think, and know

Birth must be a beautiful thing to see I
think,   and   believe
The day of birth must be a day of newness
The day of birth must be an ignition of new
hope
The day of birth must be a time of
togetherness
The day of birth must be a moment of light
Its happiness, could be naturally propelled
Its happiness, could be created by society
and   culture
Its happiness could be a blessing from God
And this is the bliss of birthday.'
"Wow Wonderful, Quamey!" said Lyren.
She was captivated by his ingenuity. The
two friends spent some time chatting,
giggling and cracking jokes to make the
best out of the day. At 1:00pm the college
bell rang to notify the students to resume
their next four hours of class for the day.
The twain hurried to the class together. On
their way, she said to him that she was

impressed by the poem, but it never did solve her question of destiny regarding birthdays.

He honestly professed that he didn't have the answers either, and was only left to hope, that someday she would discover these answers. That sort of sparked a flame in Lyren's heart to want to discover for herself what birthdays might perhaps reveal about destinies. She had begun to even think that this could lead to a discovery of an answer peculiar to not only her, but to the world as a whole.

CHAPTER 1

"Dreams have taste: it is called passion with discipline."–
The   *Bold.*
In a twinkling of an eye, flashes of diverse

thoughts mounted Lyren's mental faculty whilst she was thinking about the question of destiny as she occupied her seat in class. It occurred to her suddenly, that destiny might be something you create for yourself. She thought about the day she first entered Thess-Han College of Arts as a fresh student from her previous school, FrancLen College of Biology. She came as a student who was dissatisfied with pursuing biology. She was actually running from living her father's dream to make her a biology scholar, to align herself to her desire of becoming an English lecturer in the near future. It turned out to be a battle of choices, since she had to fight her father Mr. Newbold over this, as it were. She had never felt the joy or the natural inclination to study biology, even though she was very good undoubtedly at biology. Her father continually bothered her with the benefits of studying biology, since he believed that human life was factually based on biology. At home, she was bombarded with the merits of studying biology during breakfast, at lunch if the father happened to be there and then before bed time. Nevertheless, she felt within herself that she could not be persuaded by her father's conviction. The choice was then hers to forgo her father's conviction in biology in order to marshal her confidence to militate against his stereotypical thinking about the supremacy of biology. She really thought about this very hard. And then it suddenly dawned on her one day that biology itself appreciates variety, beauty, creativity, naturalness, versatility and appreciation of every little effort of both living and non-living   things. It was this understanding that gave her a formidable stand to convince her father finally. It happened that one day during breakfast, she wittingly used the variety of birds to explain and defend her point. She asked her father if he would love that all birds were Songbirds so that they could sing the same song to human beings everywhere. Mr. Newbold responded quickly that it would defeat the purpose of variety and beauty in the world. She shrewdly insisted that she would love that there were no variety of birds. Her father then stopped sipping the hot coffee and explained to her the importance of variety in the world. He went on to state that human beings even do not have the same voice to sing even though there could be similarities amongst certain singers. She quickly accepted her father's explanation and assured her father that she understood his point.

As if raising a new topic, she gently asked the father to consider whether there could be variety in the choices of students to study either biology or English? This really got her father to sit firmly and with a low face, because it had never occurred to him that his daughter was driving home her own point by raising the biology question on variety. Before leaving the breakfast table, her father assured Lyren that he would respond to her question before bed time. When Mr. Newbold returned from work, he confessed that he was very sorry for trying to impose his choice of biology on her. He assured her that she could pursue her desire to become an English lecturer. This affirmation from her father was suddenly an open heaven for the family. This is how come Lyren opted for transfer from FrancLen College of Biology to Thess-Han College of Arts.

It wondrously did occur to Lyren then that she had actually created her own destiny in making the choice to be transferred to Thess-Han College of Arts. It dawned on her that destiny was not cheaply bestowed on a person; one had to fight for it. This seemed to be her conclusion then, through the encounter with her father. Lyren used the ten minutes delay by the lecturer to share with Quamey the story of her father and herself. She thought it wise to seize the advantage for that purpose.

CHAPTER 2

After several hours of successive lectures, classes ended for Monday and each student hurried home by either walking with a friend, group of friends, hopping into their cars or picking a cab. Lyren loved to always walk with Quamey. Quamey thought of opening a conversation by spontaneously explaining to Lyren how he came by the poem entitled BLISS OF BIRHTDAY on his twenty-first birthday. He told her that he didn't write the poem himself, but he found the alluring words in a card sent to him on his birthday. She was sharply uneasy in herself since she longed to know who sent him such a lovely poem. It was a feeling of a little jealousy because deep inside she did not want any lady to be very close to him as she was. It was then a great relief when he noticed her facial expression as not lively; he quickly let the cat out of the bag with regard to the one who presented the gift. 'Mr. Newbold,' Quamey said, 'he sent it to me through his office agent.' He recounted that it was a big surprise to him upon realizing it was coming from her dad. In his mind and heart, it was a hopeful sign that her father appreciated their friendship. He explained to her that he did not tell her early about the parcel, because he wanted to share it with her as a surprise. Her countenance beamed with wide smiles and uncontrollable giggles. There was a spontaneous hug by the two friends, and they continued to walk on side by side.

Lyren momentarily took the opportunity to appreciate Quamey for how he had independently been of great help to her when she came to Thess-Han College of Art during the second semester. The time she came was a decisive time and she had two options, either to come the following year or work hard to justify that she could fit into the system irrespective of her late arrival. The college had no specific system to aid new students who came in the second semester. Such students were to write the final exams as if they had started with that particular year group on time.

It was Quamey who took courage to befriend Lyren by asking her to rely on him for any relevant assistance. She was grateful but too shy to ask for any help at all. He recognized this and planned to use the break time to update her on the relevant information and manner needed for the final examination. He did this for four weeks and she became confident to face the final examination. Graciously, he always spoke encouraging words to her, so it was not difficult for her to gain her self-confidence for the impending final examination. She was determined to honour their friendship by studying hard and abiding by the simple principles he shared with her. The end of the story was glorious as the two passed the final examination to move to the last and final year in Thess-Han College of Art. She was recounting this event thankfully to him. She concluded that her father got to know about his help and that might have probably been the cause of such a precious card from Mr. Newbold to him. He replied,"I   thought   so".

At the cross-road where Quamey had to take the left sidewalk of Wawasi Street, and Lyren had to take the north of the Estate Street, Lyren told Quamey that her birthday was on December 12 and she would love to see him at 7:00pm. And her father would gladly drop him home by his car after the celebration. He assured her that it was his pleasure to honour that lovely event. And since the birthday was just two days ahead, she repeated it several times to him till they parted ways. She did that as if he was a forgetful hearer. Yet, it was a silent and undeniable feeling between them that they liked each other. That is why such repetitions were entertained without comments from each other. It seemed that the repetitious reminder could go on as long as the other was willing to entertain it at the crossroad.

CHAPTER 3

That night, Quamey could not sleep. It was a beautiful moment to be part of the celebration of Lyren's birthday. He thought about the best attire to wear for the occasion, the best gift to give to her, and the best of words to say to her on that very day. This experience was not happening to him alone. In fact after supper, Lyren hurried to her room and had a flashback of what transpired between them at school during lunch time. She wished it to happen again and again, especially the joy of the conversations and the hug from each other. She also thought about how to welcome him, the right words to use, the kind of dress to wear and how he could sit by her by the arrangement of the chairs at the dining table. She thought about this as being part of her destiny, but could not firmly grasp the meaning.

Alas, the day of great expectation happened, he woke up very early to call Lyren at 6:00am to wish her a happy birthday, and assured her that he would be at the birthday celebration on time. She thanked him for that assurance. After the call, she felt like flying in the air. Her mother Mrs. Newbold noticed her joyful facial expression and assured her that her friend was welcome. She expressed thanks to her mommy by hugging her for about fifteen seconds. Her mother encouraged her to go and have her teeth brushed before her brother Noble woke up. This is because Noble is noted in the family for making it a fun to fight with his sister about who takes his or her bath first. It was a Tom and Jerry game between the siblings.

This has been their childhood fun as siblings. Lyren remembered the time Noble was twelve years old when a remarkable event drew them very close to each other as siblings. On that occasion they became more than siblings, they became the best of close friends. You know, it is possible for siblings to be in the same house and not be close friends. Her relationship with her younger brother Noble was a different one. They were siblings alright, but became the best of friends as they grew up. What happened on that occasion when he was twelve years was that she woke up that day at 8:00am whilst by 6:00 am her brother had already woken up. He did the unimaginable which earned him the admiration of his mother, won the respect of his father and won the love and care of his sister.

On that day, he quickly but silently rushed to the kitchen to clean up the utensils and tidy the place up for breakfast. He went ahead to fry eggs for breakfast and boiled water to prepare milo drink for the family. He specially toasted his sister's bread the way she really loved it to be. He worked within time so well that by 8:00am the breakfast table was set for the family. He then went on to wake his sister up by calling her by a sweet name, Darling-Lyn. She was so pleased in her soul to be woken up by such a pleasant word. This could be understood with a big smile on her face. She asked him to come for a big hug in appreciation for calling her Darling-Lyn.

Noble immediately climbed his sister's bed and gave her the long awaited hug with gratification. She quickly had her teeth brushed and went to the breakfast table. And since it was a Saturday, the whole family excused themselves from early bathing before breakfast.

Mr. and Mrs. Newbold got up from their bed few minutes later, had their teeth brushed and rushed to the kitchen after having had their first kiss for the morning. As it was the custom of Mr. and Mrs. Newbold, they always did the kitchen chore together on Saturday just to have enough time to chat and build intimacy. They were amazed and felt a new wave of tranquil feeling pendulating in them to see the kitchen work strangely done by someone and so early than usual. They quickly turned back and rushed to the breakfast table, and it was there and then that Lyren and Noble shouted, "Good morning Dad and Mom…" The parents were astounded and responded spontaneously, "Good morning sweets…" These are precious memories of how Lyren and Noble became close friends even though   siblings.

On that very day, Noble assumed the chief position for the day by giving his mother a seat first, and then his father. He served his father and mother with their Milo drinks, the bread and egg. Lyren looked on with deep admiration and love for her dear brother. This was a first class treatment from Noble just for the family. It was unexpected and could not be disputed that she might have influenced her brother to pick up this surprise treatment to the family. It was the most excellent etiquette to witness. Their mother got up to give him a big hug and said, "Thank you, Noble, for making this Saturday special!!!" Their father promised to give him a surprise gift before the day ended. His sister of course felt that she had achieved her objective of inculcating lovely family attitudes into him. She just shouted with gleefulness, "Hail Noble…"

Like the speed of light, Lyren resumed her birthday mood when the thought of Quamey came to her again that morning. She quickly went to take her bath, ironed her birthday dress and thence went to aid her mother prepare the family lunch. She also helped her mother in decorating the house for the evening birthday celebration. Her mother insightfully shared with her how to welcome people like Quamey at the birthday gathering. She went on to advise her that the first friendly step to exhibit was for her to be the first person to open the door for Quamey when he knocked at the door. She explained that it communicated an earnest desire to see him as part of the celebration. He would then naturally feel bold and welcome to the event. Further, it would make him feel accepted by the family and also feel being part of it. Lyren thought to herself that this was a good gesture towards Quamey. Mrs. Newbold admonished her daughter to put on her best smiles throughout the occasion and for the only guest and invitee to the birthday party. At 1:13pm, the family lunch was ready, and they enjoyed their meal which was fried yam and fried fish with much remembrance of previous celebrations of birthdays.

CHAPTER 4

In the morning of the birthday, Quamey commenced making everything ready for the event. By 2:00pm he had already ironed his polo shirt and pair of jeans trousers, and had finished his household chores. As the only child of his family, he conducted himself very well like a responsible young man. He was therefore trusted with almost everything in his father's household. This is because he had proved himself not to be ignorant of the affairs of his home, not negligent, but diligent, and trustworthy. At about 4:00pm, he was fully dressed up and sitting on his bed thinking about the poem to write for Lyren. He was determined not to buy a card but to write his own poem based on their friendship and put it in an envelope as a gift for Lyren. He was focused on making the poem reflect the quest to answer the question of destiny through friendship. He picked his pen and his yellow A-4 sheet to begin the poem. Holding his pen like a calligrapher, he penned the following:

FRIENDSHIP

Friendship with a friend,
Friendship with Lyren,
Friendship with a lady,
Friendship with my colleague,
Friendship with a new student,
Your friendship with me is a choice,

Your friendship with me is our decision,

Your friendship with me is a learning
lesson,
Your friendship with me has shown me
many things,
Your friendship with me has shaped me to
do many good things,

Your challenge was my assignment,
Your difficulty was my assignment,
Your fears were a call for me to inspire
you,
Your doubts were a call for me to help you
dream again,
Your illness saw me turn into a priest and

a medical doctor,

This was the call to friendship,
This was the call to understand our
choices,
This was the call to help each other,
This was the call to know each other,
And this call was our own making.

He finished writing the poem by 4:30pm. He actually had to be meticulous in his words and to make sure the poem captured the true friendship he was experiencing. He intended to convey every important message of appreciation and uniqueness of their friendship. Plus that, this was his first time of celebrating her birthday with her entire family. He could therefore not afford to be swallowed in his poem. He saw his poem to her as his first letter to her and her entire family. And as a young gentleman, he intended to demonstrate to the entire family of Lyren that he was glad to be her friend.

He set off to her house as he took the sidewalk that headed towards the Help Hospital junction and glared into the sky to have a glimpse of an imaginary twilight. The walking distance from his house to her house is approximately 26 minutes. His house was also not very far from her house. He was a prim and proper young man, and there was no way he was going to be late especially on this occasion.

CHAPTER 5

Perhaps his penchant for Lyren made it even too short a distance for him. Now, in order to occupy his thoughts with lovely things whilst walking to her house, he started recounting the first time he got the news that she was ill and couldn't therefore come to school. He could not wait to see her. He was actually uncomfortable in school whilst his good friend was ill at home. Immediately the closing bell sounded he rushed from the class and walked briskly to her house. That was the first time Mr. and Mrs. Newbold saw the amazing helper she had been testifying of at home about. Quamey was allowed to come in and have a seat. Noble, Lyren's brother, fetched him a glass of orange juice. This was a kind gesture he learnt from his sister.

Early on during the day of her illness, Lyren assured her mother that Quamey would definitely come to visit her after school. When Mrs. Newbold asked her how she could be so sure about this, she responded by saying,"I trust my friendship with him and he is a very caring person". Mrs. Newbold was very much impressed by this testimony about him. Actually, as she was telling her mother this testimony, her face somewhat beamed with health and happiness. The mother thought to herself, "If Quamey really comes today my daughter might then get better to even resume classes the next day!"

Quamey sipped the orange juice slowly and gently but meditatively, Noble rushed to his sister's bedroom to wake her up to come meet Quamey. She quickly marshaled her strength, got up from the bed and went with him. He did a lovely thing by supporting her sister a bit to descend stairs. Quamey quickly stood upon seeing Lyren descend the stairs to come meet him. He just lifted up his voice with deep compassion and said to Lyren, "I have missed talking with you..." Spontaneously, it worked like a miracle as both began to laugh uncontrollably. As she drew closer, he told her that she would be fine. She was very pleased to see him and to hear these friendly words from him. She actually felt strength in herself and saw herself in school the next day.

Mr. and Mrs. Newbold were deeply encouraged by how things had turned positively for their daughter's health. They also signaled Noble to excuse the English classmates. Noble obliged even though he desired to be part of the conversation. Lyren really wanted to have a great conversation with Quamey for a longer while, so she requested that he prayed with her. He was pleased to be the one to pray with her. This was not an unusual request because he used to pray with her as a friendly custom before both of them sat for any class test. And they always came out and up with better results. He then requested for her Bible so that he could pray from the Book of Psalms for her.

Dear Lyren was happy that Quamey boldly wanted to pray with her in the house whilst the her parents were present.

She put on a lovely facial gesture that communicated how proud she was of him, because her parents were ardent believers of the Bible and longed to relate deeply with others of like conviction. She then calmly called on her brother to fetch her Bible from her bedroom. Noble quickly did that as he also had the opportunity to appear before their presence again. He brought the Bible and slowly but reluctantly left their presence. Quamey said thank you passionately to Noble as he was leaving their presence. He decided to read some verses of the Scripture to her by turning into Psalm 91. From the New International Version(NIV) did he read as follows:

"He who dwells in the shelter of the Most High will rest in the shadow of the Almighty. I will say of the LORD, 'He is my refuge and my fortress, my God in whom I trust.'

Surely he will save you from the fowler's snare and from the deadly pestilence. He will cover you with his feathers, and under his wings you will find refuge; his faithfulness will be your shield and rampart.

You will not fear the terror of night, nor the arrow that flies by day, nor the pestilence that stalks in the darkness, nor the plaques that destroy at midday. A thousand may fall at your side, ten thousand at your right hand, but it will not come near you. You will only observe with your eyes and see the punishment of the wicked."

Lyren appreciably said Amen as she believed that the reading of the Scriptures and its contents had perfectly secured her to return to school the next day. Quamey hugged her and went to bid farewell to Mr. and Mrs. Newbold who were just at the balcony of the house. Lyren said a big thank you to Quamey for his kind visit and prayer. Noble went to open the door for him gently. Mrs. Newbold came to Lyren to assure her that she had got a good friend and everything demonstrated by him was a sign of deep likeness for her. She giggled and went to her bedroom. She thought about the whole scene again and again such that she really thought that she was not really ill but in love with him. Quamey remembered this moment of visiting Lyren at the time she was ill as he was walking to Lyren's house to be part of the birthday event. He got to the door of her house exactly 6:47pm.It was a beautiful scene as she was also close to the main door to open up to welcome him into the house. He pressed the door bell and she was right there to welcome him. The two hugged and went into the living room together. Mr.and Mrs. Newbold came to welcome him as well and sat with him for five minutes to appreciate him for being part of the celebration. Noble greeted him with wide smiles and also with a manly handshake in fondness of him. Lyren was very quiet observing how the family was welcoming her special friend. The family dog, Bingo, which usually deterred visitors from coming to the house, was at this time acting soberly. Lyren and Noble must have warned it to behave appropriately towards any visitor on that very day.

CHAPTER 6

Mr. Newbold rose to his feet and called on everybody to do likewise as he began to say a few words to everybody. They all rose up to their feet with elation and wide smiles on their faces. The dog was moving in between them wagging its tail. Mr. Newbold began by saying how he really adored his daughter Lyren. He told a story about some of her childhood events when she was seven years old. It was lovely for a father-daughter relationship. In that, Lyren at the age of seven never called her father just daddy. Lyren at the sight of her father would run to him and say "my daddy". Mr. Newbold always felt an unusual closeness to Lyren and longed to come home to see her anytime he went to work. As a result, he also planned to buy Lyren something a child would love, anytime he closed from work. In fact, most times he bought the gift on his way to work in order to package it for her lest he forgot.

What was also remarkable to Mrs. Newbold was how helpful Lyren actually was at the age of seven. Lyren loved playing in the house and helping her mother with anything she could possibly help her with. Lyren was always somehow conscious of the time 5:40pm as that was usually the time the father returned from work. She made sure she had done her homework and had taken her bath before her daddy arrived. She always wanted to be the first one to be lifted up in daddy's arms and be pecked by her daddy. And then would ask her dad if there was any surprise for her on that day. Her daddy of course always had a surprise each time for her and would say to her, 'yes my girl.' As Mr. Newbold was recalling all these events, Lyren was very happy as Quamey looked at her for a while in admiration. Mr. Newbold then said a prayer to begin the birthday celebration. He went by saying, "Dear God, we thank you for making our gathering memorably, and we praise you for letting our hearts be opened to each other to enjoy the best of today in Christ Jesus, amen." They all responded, 'Amen' to Mr. Newbold's prayer. Everybody was ushered to the dining table for the next phase of the celebration. The question of destiny dawned on Lyren again. In her mind, she was happy and at the same time saw that her birthday was coloured with the adventure of good memories of the past and appreciation.

Quamey realized that Lyren was a little bit quiet and kind of been captured by a thought in her mind. So he wittingly touched Lyren's hand, gently, and told her that when people have not settled in their hearts what destiny they held, or could create, or were liable to, they sometimes endeavoured to find the meaning of their destinies from events, occasions, or days. This statement by Quamey awakened Lyren to the occasion and she smiled back without saying a word. The desire to understand destiny never differed from the day of the young lady Lyren.This question of destiny bothered her on her birthday and the reality struck her to enquire of her destiny and its meaning. It sounded like a long exciting adventurism to be embarked on by dear Lyren. Yet, as most difficult things are serendipitously discovered or chanced upon, it settled in dear Lyren's heart to explore this wonderful event behind her 'BIRTH' with its remarkable 'DAY' on the 12th day of December, 2011 at Sam Jonah Estate, Obuasi, in Ghana, during supper at 7:30 p.m.

Mrs. Newbold was busily moving to and fro in the house and doing what she knows to do best on such occasions. As most mothers are very good at celebrating their children's special days, Mrs. Newbold, Lyren's mother said, "My dear one is celebrating this beautiful event and I can't wait to make her bask under my lovely and sublime cooking today". Mrs. Newbold remembered her baking lessons she learnt at her professional catering school after attending high school with Mr. Newbold when she was just twenty years old. Ever since that time, she had continued to bake for the neighbourhood at reasonable prices. She is well known for saturating the mornings of the community she lives in with her yummy cakes and baked biscuits. Little children could not afford going to school without passing by her house to buy their share of the cakes and biscuits. Most often, the children came with their parents who bought for the kids, got some for themselves and their colleagues at work as well.

At the catering school, Mrs. Newbold won most of the cooking contests. On one occasion, the contest involved the preparation of pancake, which was a simple assignment. Before the appropriate day, Mrs. Newbold went the extra mile to study the various possible ingredients that could be added to the preparation of pancake. For example, she discovered that there were certain flavours that could be added to the normal pancake. She found pineapple flavour to be one of the flavours that could be added to the pancake. She learnt how to do this and employed it in her   contest.

Lo and behold, it was the distinguishing effect of the pineapple flavor that put her on top of her colleagues in the contest. She was given brand new cooking utensils as the reward and allowed on that day to prepare any additional food of her choice to share with her loved ones except her colleagues. Mrs. Newbold was very happy as at that time she was courting Mr. Newbold. She saw it as an opportunity to celebrate her victory with Mr. Newbold. She prepared beef pizza in addition to the pancake. She sent the packed food through their delivery and service agency to the office of Mr. Newbold with inscription on it, "From Love to My Love." This really made the day of Mr. Newbold. It was as if the whole world had come to give him the best of gifts on earth. He quickly knew who it was from and gladly opened the gift. He was extremely happy to read the note beside the package that indicated that Mrs. Newbold was adjudged the best caterer at the cooking contest. He made sure he enjoyed the pancake and pizza alone so that he could give a better testimony about the food. Immediately after consuming the food, he phoned Mrs. Newbold and that was another chapter of expression of romance in their conversation. Such moments flooded the mind of Mrs. Newbold as she was moving to the kitchen to take charge of the final decoration of the birthday cake for Lyren.

CHAPTER 7

The family dog Bingo followed Mrs.
Newbold to the kitchen whilst wagging its
tail. Bingo was doing the amazing thing on

this day. Bingo went to the kitchen, returned to the dining table and moved around a little bit sniffing all the way through. He never behaved calmly at the sight of a visitor. Yet on this occasion, it was almost getting close to Quamey as often as it could and as many times as it could without disturbing the peace of the moment. It went to kneel beside Quamey's feet wagging its tail and expecting a possible gentle touch from him. Lyren looked on in admiration as the family dog was acting wisely on this occasion to honour her special visitor. Lyren whispered to Quamey, 'Bingo likes you now', and encouraged him to just put his hands gently on its head and caress it from there to its back which he did. Bingo was now acting like he was sleeping in response to the gentle touch of Quamey. Quamey was happy that the family dog was responding this way to him and whispered to Lyren that the dog was lovely. Lyren just giggled slyly.

Mrs. Newbold shouted from the kitchen calling aloud the name of Lyren to come over to the kitchen. She excused herself and walked briskly to the kitchen. Noble took the floor by telling Quamey and Mr. Newbold about two jokes. He started by narrating as follows; there was a girl whose boyfriend honoured an invitation of her entire nuclear family to have supper. He arrived and was given a seat. He acted politely throughout, enjoyed the meal and talked with the family very well. In the course of the conversation during the meal time, they all realized that it was too late to allow the boyfriend to go home as the snow had fallen heavily within some few minutes. The girl's father urged him to stay in the boys quarters since the family had enough room to house even five visitors. He thanked them and obliged to spend the night there. But before he went to bed, he requested that the family allow him to go home, bathe and change into his pajamas so that he could come back and spend the night there.

Quamey and Mr. Newbold started laughing uncontrollably as they saw this joke as a creative masterpiece. Noble rose up from his seat and told them he had another joke, and assured them that this one was thought provoking and very funny. He continued by saying that there was a man who wanted to make a point to his new girlfriend that he had money even though in actual fact he was poor. He dressed nicely and took the girl to the city and to one of the city's most expensive shops. He decided to do window shopping with his girlfriend whilst she was also determined to make him buy one expensive bag for her. She picked the bag and said to him please could you buy this bag for me since I forgot to take my card to withdraw money. The man also responded confidently his card had expired so she should please let the bag go and consider it another time. This got Mr. Newbold laughing loudly and calling on his wife and daughter to come and listen again to the second joke. But Lyren responded that they overhead Noble from the kitchen and so they should continue to enjoy their jokes.

CHAPTER   8

Lyren came to the dining table after helping her mother with some few other things at the kitchen. Mrs. Newbold hurriedly decorated the birthday cake with candles and got ready to bring it over to the dining room. Noble told Lyren that her day was making him wish it were his birthday celebration and moment. Suddenly, Lyren shouted joyfully at the dining table, "Wow! This is my day."Mr. Newbold was glued to his seat desiring to hear what Lyren had as the secret of her BIRTHDAY.

He longed to see Lyren take the floor of the moment since her words had been fewer than expected by him. He probably longed to see her tell them how she felt about the moment. Graciously, she cleared her throat with an excuse and proceeded by expressing how happy she was to be in her family. She appreciated her father for the care and concern he had demonstrated to her since childhood. She had plethora of precious memories of birthdays since the age of five as far as she could vividly remember. She continued by saying that she will never forget the day she was taken to the city zoo at age nine to see different kinds of animals on her birthday. She smiled about how she liked to own a particular parrot at the zoo but the bird was not for sale. She cried to have the bird but it was impossible to have the bird. She remembers what her father said to calm her down. She pointed out that her father said that the bird is always your friend and you can come here to visit your friend anytime you miss it. She was convinced by this statement and allowed the bird to remain in the cage at the city zoo. Noble giggled.

Lyren continued that she remembered on

her twelve birthday how her dear mother, Mrs. Newbold surprised her by baking a birthday cake in the shape and design of number twelve. Lyren never wanted to cut any part of the birthday cake, yet as a birthday custom she had to hold the birthday knife and cut into the birthday cake to employ the applauds of the family. She also told them about how Noble bought her a necklace on her fifteenth birthday. She smiled even as she was telling them this one because the chain was still around her neck as she was testifying about her birthday adventure. She thanked Noble again and said to Noble I love   you.

Lastly, Lyren took the opportunity to appreciate her friendship with Quamey. She told the family that Quamey had been very encouraging to her especially in her academics as he helped her to study correctly to catch up with the demands of the Thess-Han College of Art. Mr. Newbold and Noble stood up to greet Quamey for a work well done by saying thank you. Quamey was truly overwhelmed by the warm appreciation from the family. Mrs. Newbold quickly joined them from the kitchen to appreciate Quamey as well. Quamey rose to present his poem to Lyren and she was taken aback when she opened it to find out that it was a poem personally written by Quamey as her twenty first birthday gift. She said a big thank you to Quamey and hugged him boldly and lovely but for a short while. The family looked on and they said wow together.

Everybody sat on his or her chair as Lyren pleaded with Quamey to read the poem to them all. Again, he was very pleased to do that and went like this

FRIENDSHIP

Friendship with a friend,
Friendship with Lyren,
Friendship with a lady,
Friendship with my colleague,
Friendship with a new student,
Your friendship with me is a choice,

Your friendship with me is our decision,

Your friendship with me is a learning lesson,
Your friendship with me has shaped me to do many good things,
Your challenge was my assignment,
Your difficulty was my assignment,
Your fears were a call for me to inspire you,
Your doubts were a call for me to help you dream again,
Your illness saw me turn into a priest and a medical doctor,

This was the call to friendship,
This was the call to understand our
choices,
This was the call to help each other,
This was the call to know each other,
And this call was our own making.

CHAPTER 9

The whole family said that it was a beautiful poem. They congratulated Quamey for such creativity and thoughtfulness. Lyren felt like flying in the air as this was definitely going to be posted on the wall in her room. She said a big thank you to Quamey. Mr. Newbold looked on and observed the scene with admiration. He personally stood up to shake the hands of Quamey and said thank you my son. He confessed that he had been challenged to confess something to everybody which was only known to Mrs. Newbold. Mrs. Newbold herself was wondering what the confession would be.

Mr. Newbold proceeded; when I was in the high school, where I first set eyes on Mrs. Stacy Newbold, I thought of striking a rapport with her by finding out on which day her birthday fell. I discovered this by checking the high school annual magazine. I was so happy to know this and planned to make advancements toward her. On one occasion where students were supposed to participate in their various fields of interest in sports, he chose to be part of the football team of the school. He eventually ended up being the captain of his team because of his leadership ability, wisdom and ability to win people's hearts easily.

Mr. Newbold was a very good defender and was well known among his colleagues and year group by the name TRANQUILITY. This was because his presence made them feel a sense of peace in the team. It was very difficult for an opponent to bypass him and score a goal against his team. At the time his school was having their final competition with the neighbouring high school, almost every student was at the city stadium to witness the event. Mr. Newbold's team carried placards and majority of them carried placards with the inscription TRANQUILITY. This was not new to him though but the whole event assumed a different meaning for him when at a glance he chanced on Stacy holding the placard with inscription TRANQUILITY. Mr. Newbold continued by saying, at that moment I felt like playing the best game in my whole life. The game started and the opponents of Mr. Tran Newbold's team were no match for them as they still proved to be the defending high school football champions. Tranquility successfully defended the ball from passing by him to the goal in a way that almost everybody in the stadium was shouting the name TRANQUILITY during the second half of the game. The whistle was blown to end the game after forty five minutes of the second half. The students rushed to the field to carry TRANQUILITY and some few other players in the team since they had won by three goals to nil. Tran indeed stilled the storms from the opponents.

Celebrations continued immediately after the victory. Mr. Newbold sighed and continued that it was from that moment that Stacy and I got our eyes fixed on each other to become good friends. In fact, Stacy personally came to shake him and expressed how she was delighted to see him perform so well for the schools' victory. Tran remarked that it was his pleasure to do that and was most grateful to be individually appreciated by such an audacious beauty. They talked for a while and laughed a little bit before the two parted ways as Tran headed towards the dressing room. Tran kept thinking about what had transpired between Stacy and him whiles he was taking his shower in the gents' bathroom which was also in the dressing room. Mr. Newbold confessed that it was at this point that he felt like calling Mrs. Newbold during that evening when he got home. At home, he quickly took another shower and shared the team's victory with his parents since they could not come to witness the whole moment of excitement for their son. When it was 7:00 pm, he was thinking about how to introduce himself on the phone to Stacy if she picked the call. He decided to write it down and look at it whilst talking with her. By 7:35pm, he was sure that the right way to introduce himself and to engage her in a lovely conversation was well laid down on the sheet of paper in front of him. He then called and alas Stacy's father picked the call. He didn't tremble though but then he couldn't introduce himself the way he had wished to do. Yet he introduced himself anyway and Stacy's father told him to hold on.

Suddenly, Mrs. Newbold heard that her father was calling her to come and take her call. Stacy asked who it was, and he said to her that it was Newbold. Mrs. Newbold shouted "that is TRANQUILITY" and she then hurried to take the call. Mr. Newbold said that he was then relieved since he overheard her excitement as she picked the call. He quickly said hello I am Newbold. She responded I know you are TRANQUILITY. They both laughed and desired to talk about the whole football event again. He told her that he called to find out how she was doing and that he was glad to see her at the city stadium. He extended an invitation to her to have a chat together the next day at lunch time. She was pleased and said "that is alright my friend". He was glad to hear the words my friend and so he also said good bye then my very good friend, and that was the end of the call.

This was a pleasant memory running through the mind of Mr. Newbold. He remembered again that on the birthday of Mrs. Newbold during her student days he was the first person to call her early in the morning at 6:00am to wish her a happy birthday. He assured her that he had a poem for her and would get to hear it if she came to school. They met at lunch as agreed and Mr. Newbold pulled out the sheet to read the poem to her. The poem went like this:

Good Memories

Time has printed our friendship together,
Time has accepted us to be friends,
Time has blessed us with good memories,
Time has taught us to be friends side by side,
Time has made this day memorable for us,
Time has taught us to remember each other,
Time has given us a reason to continue to be friends,
Time has solved our doubts and fears of friendship,

These good memories cannot be deleted,
These good memories cannot be taken away,
These good memories are a mirror for the good future,
These good memories have made us friends in this time,
These good memories are carefully selected by destiny,

So we celebrate our friendship with joy,
So we uphold only good memories of our friendship,
So we encourage ourselves to remember our friendship,
So our hearts are full of the joy of the moment,
So I am glad today is your BIRTHDAY.

This kind of poem spiced up the friendship between Mr. and Mrs. Newbold during their high school days. After the poem he finally told her "I like you". She was very delighted and hugged him for about ten seconds and said thank you for the poem, Newbold. This was because Mrs. Newbold was overjoyed to receive such a gift from Mr. Newbold. It seemed like a love letter to her no matter the content of it. And that was the time the two of them really accepted in their hearts that they were meant for each other. These are some of the good memories that flooded the mind of Mr. Newbold when he was congratulating Quamey for the beautiful poem read to Lyren on her birthday.

CHAPTER 10

Noble also observed the whole scene and thought to himself that he could write a birthday poem from what was happening to everybody on Lyren's birthday. He observed the wide smiles on his father's face, the warm appreciation from his mother Mrs. Newbold, the comfortableness exercised by Quamey and the merry moment that was working in Lyren's heart. He believed that the day must be phenomenal and beautiful for everyone. Noble, Lyren's brother was already holding his pen to write a Christmas poem out of this secret to suit December 25th.

It was as though Lyren could read the mind of Noble, she was so happy within that she started narrating the joy of the moment softly as if telling the Santaclaus story to little children. She actually didn't know how to begin, what to say and how to go about it, yet the joy of the moment was so strong within her when she was asked to say something, she extemporaneously recited:

The songbirds errantly make it known to creation about the splendor of this day,
The splendor of this day is like beholding a rose   flower,
The day has a song for me to listen to,
The day has become a lovely songbird to me,
It is full of lovely poems and pleasant memories,
I can hear the songbirds singing to my heart,
Their voices are unique and their words are welcome in my heart today,
The wonderful songs of joy long awaited are ringing in my heart today,

Oh, there is a sweet melody in the air,
Oh, there is a sweet melody in this home
Oh, there is a sweet melody in my heart

today,
A melody which is sung by everyone here,

The songs are ringing with sweet melodies,
The hibiscus flowers are a collective bijou,
The giant trees during Christmas sing praise with their leaves,
They herald the songs of HAPPY BIRTHDAY,
They bear the news of celebrations,
They clad the moment with beauty,
They clad the moment with songs of joy,

The lullaby songs of children help us to dwell in tranquility,
Memories then become kings and queens,
Singers become stewards to renew the times of joy,
Instrumentalists become friends to produce the sweet melodies again,
Friends become the audience to celebrate with us,

Parents become the conductors to steer the moments,
Appreciating this day as a tranquil journey,
And everybody becomes the referee in their memories.

There was a loud applause from everybody as Lyren gently ended this extempore recitation of poem concerning the memories expressed by almost everybody except maybe the family dog Bingo. Quamey said to Lyren that she was indeed a good poet. Lyren assured him that it was extempore and that it was the joy of the moment that had helped her to express herself in such a lovely and touching way. She testified that she herself was touched as those words were coming from her being.

It seemed that everybody forgot that it was

getting late since there was so much to remember and celebrate. Noble, who was known in the family for going to bed early could not resist the joy and beauty of the moment. He could not trade it for sleep even though at a point he was feeling sleepy. Inasmuch as he was feeling sleepy before Lyren ended her extempore poetic speech, Noble's sleep escaped him around 8:12 p.m. whilst Mrs. Newbold also tiptoed to the kitchen to go and bring Lyren's twenty first birthday cake. In a hurry, the family dog, Bingo followed the steps of Mrs. Newbold to the kitchen. It was amazing that Bingo had remained calm during the whole night. This dog must have had a good memory of the previous birthday of Lyren and how she talked to it to behave nicely on such special occasions. It was as if a peace pact had been signed between Lyren and the family dog. This was because Bingo could not entertain visitors after 8:00pm. It was the kind of dog which was trained to act wild and protective against visitors after certain hours of the night. It suffice to say that this was a miracle induced by the imminent birthday celebration that promised Bingo pieces of cake and chicken bones, a nice treatment for it.

Previously, Bingo got everybody worried about the coming of visitors before and after 8:00pm. It therefore became known to the family of Mr. Newbold that their family dog was only friendly to the family and not outsiders nor visitors. And that to get it to behave appropriately at certain times as required must mean adopting two methods, one is to cage it before a visitor arrives or speak to it sternly with the promise of one of its favorite foods before a visitor arrives. This always worked and that was how it became a miracle to visitors who had previously been threatened by Bingo to see it behave friendly.

Furthermore, Mrs. Newbold's readiness to throw some pieces of cake to it had a catalytic effect on the family pet since she always signaled to it to follow her wherever she went to in the house, especially to the kitchen. It was comforting then to see it behave friendly, at least during this panoramic event of Lyren's birthday. Noble on observing how the family pet acted was kept on high hopes to expect a beautiful poem from the whole event at the end of the celebration. It was indeed an odyssey of precious memories and discovery of destiny to everybody.

Mrs. Newbold shouted joyfully "the cake is coming and everybody should be ready to celebrate another phase of the event."

Quamey really adored the way Mrs. Newbold was bringing the cake from the kitchen. It was the most meticulous walk he had ever seen apart from that of a soldier saluting his superior respectfully. Mrs. Newbold took her steps carefully with the birthday cake like a chorister singing the processional hymn. It was adorable to Quamey and he whispered to Lyren that he loves the aroma of the cake. This was not surprising as Mrs. Newbold was known to bake the kind of cake with an aroma which can travel to the neighbouring houses.

Noble again was kept in suspense as he continuously thought that maybe there was a taste of bliss in birthdays that only those who were entitled to embrace such days would be able to survey their innate happiness intrinsic to it. He thought of it as a kind of long adventurism! An odyssey!

Noble finally determined to sleep without further influence since he was really longing to be on his bed. He had tired himself out throughout the whole week in preparation towards his sister Lyren's birthday. He was extremely overburdened on the very day of Lyren's birthday as he took upon himself to help his mother in the preparation of the cake, washing the plates to be used for the fried rice, the glass to be used for the drinks and the mopping of the ground floor where the big dining table was   located.

The birthday celebration was centered on the dining table, and so Noble ensured thorough cleaning as Lyren employed him to do that one extremely well. Noble did a good work and did not have rest as Lyren called him upstairs for him to run some errands for her before the time of the birthday was due. He gladly did all these and was determined to make her dear sister's day very memorable. Therefore, it was neither an act of laziness nor selfishness for Noble to have felt very sleepy at the heart of the birthday celebration. He was indeed very tired.

Nonetheless, Noble's fortress of resistance was broken by a powerful weapon of Lyren's poetic speech, coaxing him to listen attentively. This time, Lyren had been thinking about it and was waiting for the moment to let the poetic words come out of her through her speech. She had been premeditating on it immediately after the first one which was extemporaneously done. The joy and success of the first one encouraged her to come up with as many poetic speeches she could possibly prepare in her heart. She said that
A ROSE FLOWER
This day has become a rose flower,

A flower not trampled upon,
A flower tender in eyes of my family,
A flower lovely in appearance to all,
A flower, birds would like to sap its nectar,
A flower, bumble bees would like to sap its nectar,

It produces the nectar of joy,
It produces the nectar of peace,
It produces the nectar of happiness,
It produces the nectar of hope,
It produces the nectar of unity,
It produces the nectar of love,
It produces the nectar of togetherness,
It produces the nectar of sweet melodies,
And we have all tasted of this nectar today,
And we have all been fed by this nectar today,
And we have all been made happy by this nectar today,
And we have all been united by this nectar today,

And we have all fallen in love with good memories of each other today,

This day has become a rose flower indeed,
A flower that is well admired,
A flower that is everybody's joy,
A flower that is everybody's expectation,
A flower nursed by my family,
A flower adorable again and again admired by my family,
A flower that reminds my mother of her successful delivery,
A flower that applauds my father's excellent responsibility,
A flower that praises my brother's humility,
A flower that draws my loved ones to shout with me a HAPPYBIRTHDAY!
Noble was quickened to rise from his seat as he began to think himself that Lyren had the secret rolling and spoke to his mind, "I better get my pen rolling evenly

along with her narration." It was even wow to him when he heard his attitude of humility being praised in the poem. At this point Lyren got the family on board emotionally by gestures and ineffable lovely smiles. The manner in which she smiled as she recited the poem made her most attractive for the occasion. Her smiles were a weapon that captivated everybody to experience this collective joy moving in the atmosphere. Her smiles smothered her father's curiosity to listen without any disturbance.

CHAPTER 11

Mr. Newbold felt like a child again at the dining table as there was a quick flashback in his precious memory regarding his twenty first birthday that ushered him into a new phase of life. In fact, it was on his twenty first birthday that he boldly started making calculated advancement towards Mrs. Newbold, now his dearest wife. It was the most adventurous day in his life. He had to learn how to understand his own emotions and that of others, precisely Mrs. Newbold. He had to discern whether the moment was that of love or infatuation. He had to make some bold and life changing decisions with regards to courting Mrs. Newbold. He had to think about his job opportunities after school and where to finally settle in order to spend most of his working days. He had to plan everything in such a way that it would include Mrs. Newbold in his plans so they would not be far away from each other after school. In a gist, he was thinking about the possibility of his future with Mrs. Newbold.

And as most young men desiring dating and courtship with a dream lady would do, he always dressed neatly, conducted himself very well in school, acted kindly towards Mrs. Newbold, and scored good marks in class. He earned a good name TRANQUILITY for his excellent football performance at school and beyond his neighbouring schools. TRANQUILITY became a household name amongst the students in the school during football competitions. Mr. Newbold was focused on having Stacy as his future wife and both won each other at long last. There was a moment that whenever Mr. Newbold greeted Stacy with big smiles and asked her how she was doing, she in turn always graciously responded to him with words like, "I like you, Newbold. You make me smile…"

Any time Tran Newbold heard those

hopeful words from Stacy, he felt like swimming from one end of the Atlantic Ocean to the other end. He felt like diving into the deep seas to harpoon a whale just for her. It was a déjà vu moment for Mr. Newbold indeed. He could not trade those words for any class lessons at school. Such words gave Tran Newbold the hope of good relationship with Stacy, and assured him of their life together after school. Mrs. Newbold at that time was herself not exonerated from this beautiful mutual sensation within her. In fact, her feelings were probably stronger than Mr. Newbold's as she used to wait for Mr. Newbold after lunch hours in school. She would then say to Mr. Newbold that she just wanted to say hi to him before the break time was over. The two of them would engage in a little conversation and sometimes exchanged their drinks as a sign of love and care for each other.

The beautiful childhood days quickly flooded Noble's mind and descended on him like a visible gorgeous angel from heaven as he watched his father so enslaved by good memories of the past. Noble at this point also caught the déjà vu fever as well. This reminded Noble of his fifteenth birthday and how Lyren sung for him the blue bird song which went like this,

Happy   birthday   to   you
Happy   birthday   to   you,
Happy   birthday   to   you,
You   are   dear   to   me,
You   are   my   darling,
You   are   my   sweetest,
You   have   big   dreams   in   life,
You   have   grace   to   do   your   part,
You   can   achieve   all   your   dreams,
Your   years   are   rich   in   glory,

Blessed are you now my brother,
Blessed are you now my brother,
For God has blessed this day for you,
Rejoice, rejoice with authentic joy,
Rejoice, rejoice with authentic joy,
For this is your day...Hahaha...

This made Noble smile gently as he felt that destiny was calling on his name to be awaken to another birthday. The undoubted feeling of love cropped up in Noble's heart helping him grasp the insight of what the birthday could mean to Lyren. This inconceivable and pleasant inner burning sensation of déjà vu was a therapy to eschew and curb Noble's sleepiness. This was soul-enriching moment of joy. It was a kind of joy full of flashback memories of birthdays and times with loved ones. It did not become Lyren's joy alone, rather the family-centered and the birthday-centered happiness.

As everybody was touched emotionally by the deep thoughts of Lyren's second poem, and the lessons the poem revealed about rose flower and how she appreciated her father, mother, brother and friends, Bingo was moving around the dining table in a lovely manner and wagging its tail as if it had also been touched emotionally. Everybody started laughing as they observed the way Bingo, the family dog finally rolled on the floor joyfully as they looked at it sternly. Mrs. Newbold had already reached the dining table and placed the birthday cake in the centre. Everybody said wow! Plates were already arranged in front of each person; a prayer was said after which Mrs. Newbold served the food and drinks. They enjoyed the fried rice and the drinks together, whilst a musical track entitled "Give Thanks" by

Don Moen was played at the background.

At 9:20 p.m., Noble breathed in the strong aroma of the birthday cake prepared by Mrs. Newbold. Noble said to himself, "This will be yummy! You can't miss it, Noble!" Dear Lyren's eyes busily gazed at the sparkling and dazzling icy birthday cake brought by Mrs. Newbold. At the sight of the cake, Lyren seemed to be prudently thinking about how the knife should dissect the cake so that this act would employ a lot of applauses, deploying the serenity of the BIRTHDAY. Such was the moment of beautiful child-like-thinking. It was like becoming a little judge and honestly weighing this eventful day joyously on the table of God's loving-kindness. It was like seeing how good God could be to her as she thought about it.

CHAPTER 12

When each person had enjoyed a large chunk of the fried rice and had had some drinks, Lyren was called upon to stand up as the family and Quamey sung the happy birthday song for her. This was the same birthday song that was sung by Lyren for Noble on his fifteenth birthday. It was a popular song for almost the youth in that

community. And so they sung,
Happy birthday to you,
Happy birthday to you,
Happy birthday to you,
You are dear to us,
You are our darling,
You are our sweetest,
You have big dreams in life,
You have grace to do your part,
You can achieve all your dreams,
Your years are rich in glory,

Blessed are you now Lyren,
Blessed are you now Lyren,
For God has blessed this day for you,
Rejoice, rejoice with authentic joy,
Rejoice, rejoice with authentic joy,
For this is your day…Hahaha…

The family shouted Happy Birthday as
Lyren simultaneously blew the lighted
candles off the cake and cut the well

decorated twenty first birthday cake at 10:00pm. The family pet Bingo, paced the floor joyfully and obviously expecting more pieces of birthday cakes thrown to it. And Mrs. Newbold was sensitive to the family pet Bingo and graciously threw more than little pieces of the cake to it. Mr. Newbold suddenly intercepted the moment by presenting a beautiful yellow dress to Lyren. This dress could make Quamey attempt to propose to her immediately. It was just a beautiful dress to behold. Lyren leaped and shouted, "Thank you, Dad!" with great elation and with wide arms to hug her father. She then proceeded lovingly to give her father, mother, Noble, and of course Quamey big pecks.

Lyren finally broke the siege of suspense when Mrs. Newbold was sharing the cake. She succinctly unearthed the secret of the odyssey behind the beauty of her birthday by saying that "one might as well know with certainty that each day is independently beautified, as in

BIRTYHDAY

Monday's child is fatherly or motherly,
Tuesday's child is a person of creativity and   impact,
Wednesday's child is heartwarming and loving,
Thursday's child is a story teller and a wonder,
Friday's child is hospitable and gracious,
Saturday's child is humble and with a loyal heart,   and
Sunday's child is full of favour and progress.
And my adventure happens on Thursday. I am a story teller! And I am a wonder!"
Everybody stood up and wondered about this third poem. It was indeed the grand

finale of all the poems of that moment. They danced, shouted and praised Lyren for such creativity.

Noble shouted, "Alas, I've got your back Lyren! I've got the Birthday odyssey poem penned down! Wow..." The family laughed heartily. Mr. Newbold blessed the night with a prayer of thanksgiving to God. Mr. and Mrs. Newbold thanked Quamey for coming. Quamey thanked Lyren and her family for inviting him and he expressed how he enjoyed the birthday celebration. Lyren in turn appreciated Quamey profusely for making her birthday memorable and sweet. They both hugged and said good night to each other. Mr. Newbold drove Quamey home.

ABOUT THE AUTHOR

FRANCIS K. OFFIN (aka The*Bold) writes poems, prose and is passionate about blessing his generation with his gifts and talents in writing. He holds a Bachelor of Arts degree in Philosophy and Study of Religions from the University of Ghana and a Bachelor of Laws degree from the same university. As part of his call, he is currently studying for a Barrister-at-Law certificate at the Ghana School   of   Law.

"Friendship is a choice of decision." – The*Bold

Offin   BIRTHDAY ODYSSEY